If Only...

2

If Only...

SERMONS FOR THE MIDDLE THIRD
OF THE PENTECOST SEASON
(SUNDAYS IN ORDINARY TIME)

**WALLACE H.
KIRBY**

SERIES C FIRST LESSON TEXTS FROM
THE COMMON (CONSENSUS) LECTIONARY

C.S.S. Publishing Company, Inc.
Lima, Ohio

IF ONLY . . .

Copyright © 1985 by
The C.S.S. Publishing Company, Inc.
Lima, Ohio

5859 / ISBN 0-89536-753-X

PRINTED IN U.S.A.

DEDICATION

To Damian, Pat, and Cam
my Avila friends

Table of Contents

Proper 21 *Joel 2:23-30* *If Only We Would* 61
Pentecost 19 *Be Open To*
Ordinary Time 26 *The Spirit . . .*

¹Common Lectionary
²Lutheran Lectionary
³Roman Catholic Lectionary

A Note Concerning Lectionaries and Calendars

The following index will aid the user of this book in matching the right Sunday with the appropriate text during the second half of the church year. Days listed here include only those appropriate to the contents of this book:

Fixed-date Lectionaries

Common	Roman Catholic	Lutheran Lectionary
Proper 12 (July 24-30)	Ordinary Time 17	Pentecost 10
Proper 13 (July 31 — August 6)	Ordinary Time 18	Pentecost 11
Proper 14 (August 7-13)	Ordinary Time 19	Pentecost 12
Proper 15 (August 14-20)	Ordinary Time 20	Pentecost 13
Proper 16 (August 21-27)	Ordinary Time 21	Pentecost 14
Proper 17 (August 28 — September 3)	Ordinary Time 22	Pentecost 15
Proper 18 (September 4-10)	Ordinary Time 23	Pentecost 16
Proper 19 (September 11-17)	Ordinary Time 24	Pentecost 17
Proper 20 (September 18-24)	Ordinary Time 25	Pentecost 18
Proper 21 (September 25 — October 1)	Ordinary Time 26	Pentecost 19

PREFACE

He had such potential as a young man. Endowed with a sparkling personality, good looks, sound business mind, and charisma, his future in that small town was assured. Then he started drinking socially and could not handle it. No one ever called him an alcoholic even when his family left him, when he lost his business, when he went from town to town, from job to job. He accumulated debts, alienated his brother and sister, and finally ended his life in an isolated motel room. If only he had never started drinking!

How many times have you and I said, "If only . . . ?"I've discovered that my hindsight is twenty/twenty. It's my foresight that gets me into difficult situations, for I am nearsighted and afflicted with astigmatism when it comes to seeing clearly the route I need to take.

I suppose Naaman and Johash, the people of Judah and Israel, the prophets Hananiah, Jeremiah, Ezekiel, Hosea, and Joel could all say, in one way or another, "If only . . . "

"If only . . . " will be the theme of these Pentecost sermons.

Naaman, commander of the army of the king of Syria, was a great man with his master and in high favor, because by him the Lord had given victory to Syria. He was a mighty man of valor, but he was a leper. Now the Syrians on one of their raids had carried off a little maid from the land of Israel, and she waited on Naaman's wife. She said to her mistress, "Would that my lord were with the prophet who is in Samaria! He would cure him of his leprosy." So Naaman went in and told his lord, "Thus and so spoke the maiden from the land of Israel." And the king of Syria said, "Go now and I will send a letter to the king of Israel."

So he went, taking with him ten talents of silver, six thousand shekels of gold, and ten festal garments. And he brought the letter to the king of Israel, which read, "When this letter reaches you, know that I have sent to you Naaman my servant, that you may cure him of his leprosy." And when the king of Israel read the letter, he rent his clothes and said, "Am I God, to kill and to make alive, that this man sends word to me to cure a man of his leprosy? Only consider, and see how he is seeking a quarrel with me."

But when Elisha the man of God heard that the king of Israel had rent his clothes, he sent to the king, saying, "Why have you rent your clothes? Let him come now to me, that he may know that there is a prophet in Israel." So Naaman came with his horses and chariots, and halted at the door of Elisha's house. And Elisha sent a messenger to him, saying, "Go and wash in the Jordan seven times and your flesh shall be restored, and you shall be clean." But Naaman was angry, and went away, saying, "Behold, I thought that he would surely come out to me, and stand, and call on the name of the Lord his God, and wave his hand over the place, and cure the leper. Are not Abana and Pharpar, the rivers of Damascus, better than all the waters of Israel? Could I not wash in them, and be clean?" So he turned and went away in a rage. But his servants came near and said to him, "My father, if the prophet had commanded you to do some great thing, would you not have done it? How much rather, then, when he says to you, 'Wash, and be clean'?" So he went down and dipped himself seven times in the Jordan, according to the word of the man of God; and his flesh was restored like the flesh of a little child, and he was clean.

Then he returned to the man of God, and he and all his company, and he came and stood before him.

(2 Kings 5:1-15ab)

2 Kings 5:1-14

Proper 12 (Common)
Pentecost 10 (Lutheran)
Ordinary Time 17 (Roman Catholic)

If Only We Would Do The Obvious . . .

Ann, a new member of our church, gave the outward appearance of having her life all together. Tall and good-looking, she dressed well, was extremely neat, and seemed secure in pursuing an advanced degree after some years of teaching. She immediately became active in the life of the church and was especially gifted in creating excitement in some of the programs. The staff was concerned about overloading her with responsibilities, but her graciousness in accepting them and the efficient manner in which she executed them made us eager to approach her with requests.

When she asked for an appointment with me, I thought it might be to talk about her concern that her heavy involvement in the church was a deterrent to her graduate studies. It turned out that Ann wanted to know how she could enhance her relationship with God. She was disciplined in her devotional and prayer life, in her attendance at Sunday church school and church, because, as she said, "That is what a Christian is supposed to do," but, at times, she felt alienated from God.

I suggested biblical readings that would give insight into God's pursuit of us and his love for us, and other books that I had found to be personally helpful when I sensed that feeling of alienation. With some of these Ann experimented, but only on a short term basis.

I realized, after three or four sessions with Ann, that she was trying to decide if she could trust me with deeper things. I allowed her to move at her own pace, never trying to force her to reveal anything about which she felt the slightest hesitancy.

We moved from theology to some of her personal feelings about relationships and people, especially her parents. Ann finally told me that she had been seeing a psychiatrist for a number of years. "Does your doctor know you are talking with your minister?" I asked. Being an honest person, she had told the doctor, who rather indifferently agreed to our weekly sessions for "they would be harmless."

In our conversations, Ann kept coming back to her feelings about her parents. She told me how she felt that she had not been wanted or loved since she was four years old. She had gathered at that young age that her folks had only planned for one child, and her birth a few years after her sister's was an interference. Ann did not dream this up, she said, for her mother had verbalized it. As a consequence, she had been striving for some twenty years to excel in everything she did to prove that she was worthy of her parents' love and acceptance. In the process, she began to build up disgust and even hatred for anything that interfered with her goal. She tried to be perfect and demanded that same perfection of everyone else: her parents, her students, her acquaintances, and even strangers she encountered. When they could not measure up to her standard of perfection, she turned her bitterness upon them, the same bitterness she heaped on herself for failing to be perfect.

Ann was so afraid of being controlled, especially by her parents, that she read control into any overtures they made. She also interpreted inquiries and expressions of interest from others as their attempts to control her. Thus she alienated herself from groups whenever any questions were asked. She wanted desperately to be loved, and yet felt so unworthy of *being* loved that she had convinced herself that even God could not love anyone as despicable as she.

At every session, Ann made some reference to her parents. One time she had had a "disgusting" letter, another time a "manipulative" telephone call. She viewed an invitation to come home for a visit or a holiday as an interference. When her parents sent food or money, Ann said that was their way of trying to control her. "Why can't they leave me alone!" she would cry, as her face twisted into a frown.

"Don't you know why they can't?" I asked.

"I know what you want me to say," she would respond. "You want me to say that they love me. But they have to because any decent parent loves its child.''

"No, they don't have to love you, Ann. You've been out of graduate school for over a year. You still have not found a job. You have no income and they are hundreds of miles away, and they are concerned about your secluding yourself. That's why your mother writes you every week. That's why your parents want to come or help you in any way possible. They love you, and, in spite of what happened in the past, you must forgive them for their mistakes.''

"If I give them the slightest opening, they'll move right in and take control. I hate them both and will be glad when they are dead.''

Finally, I told Ann she'd never find wholeness until she forgives her parents and becomes reconciled to them.

She keeps coming, and she keeps looking at me with disbelief whenever I say that, as if she knows there must be some other way to clear up her misery.

Naaman must have had the same bewildered look when the prophet Elisha told him simply to wash in the Jordan River to be cured of leprosy.

Naaman, the highly respected and esteemed commander of the Syrian army, was certainly aware of his dreadful problem. He was willing to follow the suggestion of a household servant, that he go to an Israelite prophet for a cure. He set off with an official letter of reference from the king of Syria, and plenty of cash to pay for the services he would receive. The ten talents of silver and the six thousand shekels of gold would have translated into approximately $80,000 of our cash. We have no estimate of the retail value of the ten festal robes he took along. None of this would be reimbursed by health insurance. Naaman was willing to pay for the cure.

We can understand how he felt about Elisha's prescription. He had come a long way, and had a confusing experience with the inept king of Israel. When he finally arrived at the prophet's house, Elisha didn't even see him personally. He sent his receptionist out with the utterly absurd suggestion that Naaman take seven baths in the Jordan River.

Naaman considered this an insult to him and to his terrible problem. A problem like his deserved a more dignified solution, at least one a bit more religious. Naaman was outraged.

I thought that he would at least come out to me, pray to the Lord his God, wave his hand over the diseased spots, and cure me! I

*could have washed in better rivers back home, if muddy water is
all it takes to cure leprosy. (2 Kings 5:11)*

It was rather like going to a professional about a weight problem
and being told simply to eat less for help with obesity, or being instructed in a smoking clinic not to purchase or bum any more
cigarettes. It can't be, or at least it must not be, *that* simple. Answers that seem too simple make us feel cheated for some reason.

A woman went to her minister for help. "I have a terrible
problem getting out of bed each day. Can you suggest something
spiritual that will help me?" she asked. "I can offer you little spiritual
counseling for that problem," he replied. "But I can suggest that
you simply put one leg over the edge of the bed each morning and
then pull the other leg after it. That will put you on your feet for
the day." She was not too pleased with his counsel.

Do we think our complex, all-consuming problems deserve more
personal attention, more time from the problem-solvers, than any
simple solutions they might offer? Or do they demand more of us?

As our lives become more complicated and the issues more confusing, our problems proliferate. We may need help, and may desperately want it, but our self-image, our lack of receptivity, or our plain
misplaced pride put the very help we seek beyond us. Sometimes we,
like Naaman, are really looking for help, yet we close ourselves to
all but new answers, or sophisticated answers, or popular answers,
or answers that will do justice to the breadth and depth and width
and length of our problems. Or even worse, we sometimes look for
answers that will not only solve our problems, but will also punish
our adversaries, somehow giving us "the pound of flesh" we feel
we deserve for our suffering.

Naaman, I feel confident, was forever grateful to those servants
who talked him into taking Elisha's suggestion. They made him realize that his refusal was unreasonable, and would prevent his being
cured.

If only you will do the obvious thing, you will be cured.

And when Naaman washed himself seven times in the Jordan,
his flesh became healthy and firm.

If only Ann could do the obvious thing, forgive her parents and
accept their love, so she can be healed of her bitterness and alienation.

If only all of us would learn to forgive, and to simply accept the
love and wholeness God offers . . .

Now when Elisha had fallen sick with the illness of which he was to die, Joash king of Israel went down to him, and wept before him, crying, "My father, my father! The chariots of Israel and its horsemen!" And Elisha said to him, "Take a bow and arrows"; so he took a bow and arrows. Then he said to the king of Israel, "Draw the bow"; and he drew it. And Elisha laid his hands upon the king's hands. And he said, "Open the window eastward"; and he opened it. Then Elisha said, "Shoot"; and he shot. And he said, "The Lord's arrow of vioctory, the arrow of victory over Syria! For you shall fight the Syrians in Aphek until you have made an end of them." And he said, "Take the arrows"; and he took them. And he said to the king of Israel, "Stroke the ground with them"; and he struck three times, and stopped. Then the man of God was angry with him, and said, "You should have struck five or six times; then you would have struck down Syria until you had made an end of it, but now you will strike down Syria only three times."

So Elisha died, and they buried him.

(2 Kings 13:14-20a)

2 Kings 13:14-20a

If Only We Would
Be Disciplined . . .

"That's what we need for the kitchen," Mary whispered to her husband, Carl.

The table, among other pieces of furniture, was to be auctioned off to the highest bidders. No one thought that anything coming out of the old farm house had much value. Like Mary, the other bidders were there to supplement the furnishings of their summer cottages in the mountains of western North Carolina.

"I'll start the bidding off and won't go too high," she continued to whisper. Mary did not want the auctioneer or any potential buyer to know how interested she was in the table.

The auctioneer evidently thought the table worthless. The legs had been beaten up, perhaps by someone carelessly pushing back a chair or bench. It was a horrible black color, and there was a crack in the wooden top. Instead of starting with his customary minimum bid, the auctioneer moved toward the table and blurted out, "What will you give me for this old table?"

"Fifty cents," Mary said with as casual a tone in her voice as she could muster. She chuckled to herself at the ridiculous bid and waited to hear someone come up with at least a ten-dollar offer to top hers. The crowd, however, was apparently just as disinterested as the auctioneer, for no one offered to go higher.

"Sold to the lady for fifty cents!"

Hardly able to believe her luck, Mary paid her money while Carl went to borrow a truck. As they were loading the table, the auctioneer came over with two benches. "These were supposed to be sold with the table," he said.

"What do you want for them?" the buyers inquired.

"Oh, nothing. Just take them along. I'll throw them in with the table."

Mary and Carl took their fifty-cent purchase to their cottage, placed the table and benches in the kitchen by the windows, covered the table with a piece of oil cloth, and there they sat for their family meals for the next thirty-five years.

The cottage was sold ten years ago, and since the heirs had no place for the table and benches, they were included in the sale, and our family now sits on the free benches around the fifty-cent table.

Two summers ago, while vacationing at our log cabin, I decided to see what kind of wood was under that black paint. I started with one of the benches, and took the easy way of working on the top.

I worked on the top of that bench for two days. My first application of paint remover took part of the black away, revealing a hideous green color. After three more heavy doses of remover, plus a lot of scraping, I hit a thick, thick coat of white paint, which must have been the original covering, for the white had seeped through every grain of that wood. When I finally got all the paint off the top, I cleaned it with furniture refinisher and discovered a beautiful piece of wood. That was enough to convince me that the project would be worthy of my efforts.

Having done the easy part, I then had to do the legs of the bench. That was not exciting at all. The years of wear had smoothed the top, but the legs were rough. All that black and green and white paint had to be removed, and I had to turn that bench every way under the sun in order to clean not only the two end legs, but also the braces that made it sturdy.

"You ought to treat yourself to the table top," I thought to myself as I pulled the second bench into my workshop. "That would be nice and easy compared to what you've been doing. At least put off these bench legs until later."

I knew I had to develop some kind of discipline if I were to finish that job before the vacation ended. So I went ahead with the legs of that second bench, and worked off and on for days before getting to the top. I never allowed myself the excitement of refinishing until I had removed all the paint. When I finally got to the table, the top was made of two broad slabs of wood, and it took almost more discipline than I could muster to finish stripping and cleaning the legs before doing the top.

When I started my task I wanted quick results. I wasn't sure I wanted to suffer through all the agony of scraping and steel-wooling and sanding, especially using vacation time to do it. I made myself spend a few hours each day to make sure I finished with the difficult parts before the easier ones. Two days before we packed to go home, we ate our first meal on a beautiful wooden table and sat on two priceless antique benches. Mary's fifty-cent purchase would bring at least a five-hundred-dollar bid now.

I've had a lot of experiences that have taught me about discipline. I used to think of discipline as rules, regulations, commands, orders. It conjured up a feeling of duties that were unpleasant, disagreeable, offensive. It also meant punishment for things done or things left undone.

"This is going to hurt me worse than it will you," were the most meaningless words I ever heard my mother *utter,* and they always preceded the punishment I was about to receive. I knew, when I was told to go into the backyard and get a switch from the pear tree that, just before that switch hit my legs, Mother was going to say something about her pain being more severe than mine. I would sometimes suggest that I would be willing to forget the switching to save her from suffering. I can assure you that I deserved the switching, and it was effective because it made me realize that my lying, my backtalk, and my fussiness would destroy me. My mother's discipline was saving me from destroying myself.

The Old Testament writers felt that the nation of Israel suffered political and military defeats because of its disloyalty to God. Their accounts describe such defeats as "God's wrath," but even in the worst times, they were careful to make clear that God would never abandon his people. The purpose of his "wrath" was to discipline them and keep them from destroying themselves. The Israelite kings depended on the prophets to invoke God's blessing and to interpret God's actions.

One of those prophets was Elisha. There are some interesting accounts of his ministry scattered throughout the Second Book of Kings. Today's reading tells of Elisha's death and his final visit from Jehoash, king of Judah. When he saw the dying prophet, the king broke down and wept. "You are the strength of Israel," he cried, wondering how his nation would carry on without Elisha's prophetic leadership.

To comfort Jehoash, Elisha told him to shoot one arrow out the east window. When Jehoash did, Elisha said, "You are the Lord's arrow, with which he will win victory over Syria." (18:17, TEV)

The prophet then instructed the king to pick up the other arrows and strike them on the floor. Jehoash did as he was told, but Elisha was angry when he only struck the floor three times.

"You should have struck five or six times," Elisha exclaimed, "and then you would have won complete victory over the Syrians; but now you will defeat them only three times." (18:19, TEV)

The king must have known that striking the floor with the arrows was symbolic of the defeats of Syria. His failure to persist indicated to Elisha that Jehoash had neither the will nor the character to be Judah's leader.

The Scriptures tell about people who were willing to discipline themselves and thus become God's instruments. It also realistically relates accounts of those who were undisciplined and failed. That's true of the patriarchs and prophets of the Old Testament. It's true of the leaders of the New Testament. It's true of Jesus himself, for he decided at the beginning of his ministry, when he went through the wilderness temptations, that he would be disciplined; he would not succumb to the enticing detours of bringing in the Kingdom by self-indulgence, or power, or magic.

All of us who are serious about our commitment must be disciplined. I remember what happened in elementary school when the teacher left the room. We became unglued. Pandemonium reigned supreme. We played "catch" with the chalkboard erasers, and whizzed them across the classroom with the speed of lightning. Some of us accomplished the feat of being able to stand on our heads on top of the desks. We went about all this very quietly so that we would not be heard. Every one of us knew, however, that we never learned anything that way. In fact, we secretly longed for the teacher to return so that order would be restored. It was only in the disciplined order of the classroom that learning could take place.

A member of our church asked me to help her strengthen her relationship with God. My advice was very simple: develop a disciplined devotional life. "Spend part of each day reading the Bible in a systematic way, and then write your prayers," was the specific guidance I offered.

Three years later she wrote me a letter:

I came to you for guidance that day. As I left I felt that I was not much better off than when I came. I was looking for an instant solution to a closer walk with God. Since that time I have had a daily quiet time. I have written my thoughts and prayers. I have read, and through Bible study, I have more knowledge and insight. One day I read this sentence in a book you gave me: "If we are faithful to our discipline, a new hunger will be made known. This new hunger is the first sign of God's presence!" (Henry Nouwen, Making All Things New). *Tears ran down my cheeks, and I felt like shouting. I am on the right track. Thank you for starting me.*

Discipline is the very essence of religion, and it is also the very heart of all true happiness. If only we would be more disciplined . . .

*The word that came to Jeremiah from the Lord:
"Arise, and go down to the potter's house, and there I
will let you hear my words." So I went down to the potter's house, and there he was working at his wheel. And
the vessel he was making of clay was spoiled in the potter's hand, and he reworked it into another vessel, as it
seemed good to the potter to do.*

*Then the word of the Lord came to me: "O house
of Israel, can I not do with you as this potter has done?
Says the Lord. Behold, like the clay in the potter's hand,
so are you in my hand, O house of Israel. If at any time
I declare concerning a nation or a kingdom, that I will
pluck up and break down and destroy it, and if that nation, concerning which I have spoken, turns from its evil,
I will repent of the evil that I intended to do to it. And
if at any time I declare concerning a nation or a kingdom that I will build and plant it, and if it does evil in
my sight, not listening to my voice, then I will repent of
the good which I had intended to do to it. Now, therefore, say to the men of Judah and the inhabitants of
Jerusalem: 'Thus says the Lord, Behold, I am shaping
evil against you and devising a plan against you. Return,
every one from his evil way, and amend your ways and
your doings.' "*

(Jeremiah 18:1-11)

If Only We Would Let God Mold Us . . .

"John's pulling his ear again," my wife would say wearily when I came home for lunch. "I guess I'd better take him back to Dr. Byrd's this afternoon before things get worse."

"That probably means another round of penicillin shots for John and some more sleepless nights for us," was my usual response.

That dialogue was repeated over and over in our household. It seemed as though we would never get our three-year-old son's ear infections cleared up. We were positive his body was working up an immunity to antibiotics, because each bout with his ears meant at least three and sometimes five injections. Dr. Byrd, our family physician, must have felt the same way, for he decided John needed to be seen by a specialist.

John was excited about a trip to the city, but not about another doctor probing around in his tender ears.

"Your son needs to have tubes put in both ears so that the fluid building up behind the drum can drain. Unless this is done, he will continue to have ear infections and his hearing might be impaired."

Dr. Pope explained the surgical procedure and the necessity of a two-day stay at the hospital.

"I wish I could guarantee," he continued, "that this one time would do it. There is always the possibility of having to repeat the procedure when John is older."

The necessary arrangements were made for John to be admitted to the hospital the next week, and we went home with the tremendous task of explaining to a three-year-old child why his ears must hurt more right now so that they could get well and stop hurting altogether.

Adults who understand the necessity and value of surgery still dread it when they have to face it. How much more frightening it must be to a child who does not understand why the pain is necessary to save his life, or in this case, his hearing. He fears, in fact, that the "bad doctor" only wants to hurt him, and he cannot comprehend why his parents have betrayed him by handing him over to suffering.

How hard it was for us to explain to John that we were going to see that he went through his operation because we loved him. We tried to help him realize that the surgery he was to undergo would stop his earaches and penicillin shots. Our efforts, plus a child's book about going to the hospital, and loving attention from his older brother and sister prepared John for his ordeal.

That was nineteen years ago. John never again had to undergo the procedure, and now our twenty-two-year-old college senior has no earaches, but rather a keen sense of hearing.

Jeremiah, out of an everyday experience, tried to explain to his people how Yahweh would use their suffering to mold them, to help them become the whole persons their creator envisioned. The prophet felt led to go to the potter's house. There he watched the craftsman working at his wheel, shaping and reshaping lumps of clay, until they turned into objects of beauty. Jeremiah must have wondered why the artist would often start over again with a pot or jar that looked perfect to the observer. We can imagine that the sensitivity of the potter's eye and fingers awed the prophet, and that he was deeply impressed by the potter's control over the clay as he molded and remolded it over and over again. As Jeremiah watched, he recognized the parallel between the potter and God, the clay and the people of Judah.

"Don't I have the right to do with you people of Israel what the potter did with the clay?" Jeremiah heard God say. (18:1, TEV)

The story of the potter was written about 600 B.C. when Judah had a weak king, Jehoiachin, and had fallen under foreign domination. Within a few years the monarchy, which had begun four hundred years earlier with Saul and David, would cease to exist. The Babylonian captivity had begun. It was the worst tragedy the Israelites had ever known.

Jeremiah did not stop preaching that Judah would be destroyed, but from that day on there began to be a new hope in his message. Yahweh had shown him that destruction was not the final word. Judah was the clay and God was the Potter, a potter of infinite resourcefulness. The clay, though it be marred, could be salvaged. The wheel kept on turning and the Potter kept shaping and reshaping the clay over and over again. Judah was still in God's hands. Jeremiah began to look for and to build for a future of hope.

The picture God presents through Jeremiah is brief and simple, and extraordinarily rich. The parable still speaks to us today. Each of us is clay in the Potter's hands, just as surely as Judah was. God designs the vessel — the person each of us is created to become — in his mind. It does not even know what is to be made of it. A vase? A pitcher? A candlestick? Only the Potter knows!

Once we have learned to accept the fact that God is the Potter and we willingly yield ourselves to him, as the clay gives itself to the potter, what happens to us? It would be nice to be able to say that we have reached our goal and are ready to be fully possessed by God. The truth is that we are just now ready to begin to let God shape and mold us.

That's when our prayer life deepens, and we become more and more aware that clay can do virtually nothing to transform itself into an object of beauty. It can be soft, pliable, sensitive to the potter's touch, and allow God to shape and reshape it, even though that process can be as painful as John's surgery. We are often afraid that God's will may break us, that what he asks is too hard for us to bear. Judah felt that way when Jeremiah advised her leaders that Yahweh would allow the Babylonian captivity, and that the people should submit to the foreigners.

The clay, however, is never broken by anything the potter may do, unless it becomes hard and rigid, as John's hearing was in no danger, unless we refused to let him have tubes put in his ears. As long as it is malleable, the clay will never break, but once it begins to resist the potter's touch, to push against his shaping, it will be in danger. That is what happened to Judah and that is why God sent Jeremiah to tell her that she needed to be broken in order to be refashioned.

So it is with us. We are misshapen at times by our own willfulness and stubbornness. By our sinfulness we distort the image of God in us and become hardened to his will. As long as we are content with our shape, the attempts of the Potter to refashion and transform us will threaten and frighten us. As we begin to realize what we really are and what we might be, we will no longer dread the necessary remolding, even though it may be painful. We will find ourselves willing to be broken and remolded, because we long with all our hearts to become like the Lord of love.

Irenaeus, one of the early church fathers, wrote about our being the work of God. He advises: "Keep thy heart soft and pliable for Him; retain the form in which the Artist fashioned thee, having moisture in thyself, lest, becoming hard, thou shouldest lose the marks of His fingers."

The potter and clay image has caught the imagination of many through the years. One was Adelaide A. Pollard who wrote the beloved hymn, "Have Thine Own Way, Lord." She pictured the ideal response to God as a willingness to be molded according to the divine design.

> *Have thine own way, Lord!*
> *Have thine own way!*
> *Thou art the potter;*
> *I am the clay.*
> *Mold me and make me*
> *After thy will,*
> *While I am waiting*
> *Yielded and still.*

If only we would let God mold us . . .

O Lord, thou has deceived me,
and I was deceived;
thou art stronger than I,
and thou hast prevailed.
I have become a laughingstock all the day;
every one mocks me.
For whenever I speak, I cry out,
I shout, "Violence and destruction!"
For the word of the Lord has become for me
a reproach and derision all day long.
If I say, "I will not mention him,
or speak any more in his name,"
there is in my heart as it were a burning fire
shut up in my bones,
and I am weary with holding it in,
and I cannot.
For I hear my whispering.
Terror is on every side!
"Denounce him! Let us denounce him!"
say all my familiar friends,
watching for my fall.
"Perhaps he will be deceived,
then we can overcome him,
and take our revenge on him."
But the Lord is with me as a dread warrior;
therefore my persecutors will stumble,
they will not overcome me.
They will be greatly shamed,
for they will not succeed.
Their eternal dishonor
will never be forgotten.
O Lord of hosts, who triest the righteous,
who seest the heart and the mind,
let me see thy vengeance upon them,
for to thee have I committed my cause.
Sing to the Lord;
praise the Lord!
For he has delivered the life of the needy
from the hand of evildoers.

(Jeremiah 20:7-13)

Jeremiah 20:7-13

Proper 15
Pentecost 13 (L)
Ordinary Time 20 (RC)

If Only We Would Hold On . . .

"Staying in school is too much for me right now," Evelyn began.

As her supervising pastor, I could understand the pressures she was under. She and her husband were both in their first year of seminary, and, on top of classes, he had just been appointed to serve a two-point charge. Bill and Evelyn were conscientious young people and wanted to give their best to their studies and to their church members.

"I need some time to back away and get a new perspective on my life," she continued. "I still feel a call to ministry, but I need some relief from all the pressures. One of us in seminary right now is about all we can handle."

Who of us has not at some time felt overwhelmed by our duties and responsibilities? A boy trudging a school thinks of the fishing stream and the prospect of the schoolroom takes on a prison-like quality. The young wife, bored by her household duties and worn out by petty demands, thinks of the comparative freedom of her unmarried sisters, and feels frustrated by her own routine. The office worker, tied to a desk, gazes at the colorful pictures of vacation resorts and longs for the day when he no longer has to punch a time clock or catch the 7:59 commuter. The city-dweller grows weary of the noise and confusion of urban life. The farmer's son fumes at the demands of his chores. And so it goes with most of us!

We may want to get away from a job or other responsibilities because we are weary, bored, lazy, afraid, or desperate. Sometimes it is just a passing mood. At other times it is more serious, as it was for Evelyn that morning.

This longing to step back and take a look at one's life is a frequent theme for the biblical writers. One who expressed it poignantly and faced it openly is the prophet Jeremiah.

Jeremiah was a modest, sensitive young man. His father was a priest who served a parish in Anathoth, a suburb of Jerusalem. Young Jeremiah lived a quiet life, enjoying the obscurity and security it afforded. He did not want to be a public figure.

Something happened which brought Jeremiah out of his seclusion. Josiah, king of Judah during Jeremiah's youth, ordered repairs made on the temple at Jerusalem. During the excavation and restoration, the workers found the book known to us as Deuteronomy. When King Josiah heard the book read, he began a reform which swept through the country. The contents of this book awakened the king and the people to all the idolatrous and unethical practices into which they had fallen. Young Jeremiah was caught up in the reform, and his spirit was gripped by what he interpreted as the Spirit of God.

Jeremiah reluctantly began his prophetic career. In a sermon which he preached in the courtyard of the temple (7:1-15), Jeremiah flatly declared that both the city and temple would be destroyed. What made that sermon even harder to take was that Jeremiah said the destruction was not coming from Judah's enemies, but from God, who had chosen them and set them apart from all other people.

To the Judeans, the temple was synonymous with worship. They believed it was the dwelling place of God. It could not be destroyed. For Jeremiah to say this was like saying that God would destroy himself.

Jeremiah told the people they were bringing this destruction on themselves. Essentially he was saying, "You reformed your worship, but you failed to reform your conduct. You worship God in the temple, but you are not true to him in your heart."

"Look, you put your trust in deceitful words," he declared. "You steal, murder, commit adultery, tell lies under oath, offer sacrifices to Baal, and worship gods that you had not known before. You do these things I hate, and then you come and stand in my presence, in my own Temple, and say, 'We are safe.' " (7:8-10)

That sermon stirred up the crowd. People brought the princes and priests to hear for themselves what Jeremish was saying. They cried treason and wanted the prophet put to death. Jeremiah did escape with his life, but was re-arrested and thrown into prison numerous times. Most of his thirty years of active public life were spent either in hiding or in prison.

With all this opposition, there is little wonder that Jeremiah has been referred to as the weeping prophet. He had something to cry about. The priests opposed him; even his own father turned against him. The princes sought his life, the people called him a traitor, and his captors declared that he was a deserter.

Like Evelyn and, indeed, like most of us, Jeremiah fought with himself. The image he had of himself did not measure up to his image of a prophet of God. (1:4-10) He complained that his hearers ridiculed him because the Lord's Word, which he proclaimed, never seemed to come to pass. (17:15) He was human enough to pray that God would bring disaster upon those who opposed him. (17:16)

At times, Jeremiah felt that God had deceived him. (20:7) He told God what he was struggling with, and how tired he was of it all, but concluded that he knew God was on his side and would support him regardless of how he felt.

Even in her decision to withdraw temporarily from seminary, Evelyn, too, felt supported by God. "I still feel a call to ministry," she declared. Some weeks later when she appeared before a district committee on the ordained ministry, she affirmed her commitment to answer that call.

Both Jeremiah and Evelyn held on when the going was tough. If only we could hold on when our days are dark and the way is not clear!

Difficult days have a way of making us stronger, don't they? Difficult decisions have a way of helping us weigh matters more carefully. I feel that even our questions and doubts about the faith have a way of strengthening it and deepening our commitment to God.

Edna Ferber, in her book, *So Big,* pictured a woman sent out to the eastern prairies during the early settlement of our country. In her struggles against the hardships of a settler, she developed a sturdy noble character. Her son, relying on the money she had accumulated, sought an easier life. He tried first one thing and then another, leaving each job whenever he got tired of it. One day the mother confronted her son openly. She told him that if he had stood up to things when they were hard, his resistance would show in his hands and his face, but because he always took the line of least resistance, she said, "You are just too smooth."

Jeremiah was worn out and badly hurt by the hardships he endured. He felt free enough with God to tell him how he felt and yet, even as he complained, he knew that God's strength and might would help him to hold on.

Whenever we hold to our convictions against all odds, we develop a firmer inner core. Saint Paul testified to that: "Suffering produces endurance, and endurance produces character, and character produces hope, and hope does not disappoint us." (Romans 5:3, RSV)

I heard of a young minister who had a parish where the people seemed to resist every effort he made to minister to them. They did not appreciate his attempts to beautify the church and make the worship services more meaningful. They opposed him at every turn, and almost broke his heart. Then he was invited to a better parish. The young preacher was tempted to take it, but deep down he felt that his divine duty was to stay in that place. He did. He held on, and when things began to change, his ministry became tremendously fruitful.

Jeremiah's word for us is to hold on. He tells us not to give up. We have to be realistic and face facts, as he did. We have to admit that times get tough and things may not always be looking good for us, but we are not alone.

There are some programs today that carry a message of encouragement and hope to people in despair, and help them to hold on. Alcoholics Anonymous, "I Can Cope," and "One Day At A Time" offer a helping hand to people who are desperately ill with drug addiction or cancer. The church of Jesus Christ gives us all reassurance and promise when we are tempted to buckle under problems that overwhelm us.

We need to hear Jeremiah's word to hold on when we consider the condition of our world. How easy it is to be filled with despair at the trouble in the Middle East and in Central America. How easy it is to feel helpless and hopeless when we think of unemployment and hunger and nuclear armament. Nevertheless, we can hold on with faith, because this is still our Father's world, and "though the wrong seems oft so strong, He is the ruler yet."

If only we would hold on . . .

In that same year, at the beginning of the reign of Zedekiah king of Judah, in the fifth month of the fourth year, Hananiah the son of Azzur, the prophet from Gibeon, spoke to me in the house of the Lord, in the presence of the priests and all the people, saying, "Thus says the Lord of hosts, the God of Israel: I have broken the yoke of the king of Babylon. Within two years I will bring back to this place all the vessels of the Lord's house, which Nebuchadnezzar king of Babylon took away from this place and carried to Babylon. I will also bring back to this place Jeconiah the son of Jehoiakim, king of Judah, and all the exiles from Judah who went to Babylon, says the Lord, for I break the yoke of the king of Babylon."

Then the prophet Jeremiah spoke to Hananiah the prophet in the presence of the priests and all the people who were standing in the house of the Lord; and the prophet Jeremiah said, "Amen! May the Lord do so; may the Lord make the words which you have prophesied come true, and bring back to this place from Babylon the vessels of the house of the Lord, and all the exiles. Yet hear now this word which I speak in your hearing and in the hearing of all the people. The prophets who preceded you and me from ancient times propohesied war, famine, and pestilence against many countries and great kingdoms. As for the prophet who prophesies peace, when the word of that prophet comes to pass, then it will be known that the Lord has truly sent the prophet."

(Jeremiah 28:1-9)

If Only We Could Trust The Silence . . .

"Please try to help Steve understand that he is not going to get well," she would whisper before she opened the door to his bedroom.

"I'll try again," was the only promise I could make her.

That was about all the conversation we could have if Steve were not asleep when I went to their home on my bi-weekly visits. He would be calling out, "Who's at the door?" even before Mrs. Stone could get through the living room. His keen sense of hearing would pick up our voices whenever I'd slip in the back door to lend some support to his wife before seeing him.

We both were aware that Steve understood his condition. The diagnosis was clear. The cancer in his lungs was so advanced when he finally went to a doctor that it was inoparable, and radiation or chemotherapy would have only added to his misery. Fortunately there was little pain. Steve's laborious breathing and his weakening condition were the only outward signs of his sickness. He had been sent home to die.

Steve knew this and I was not going to force him to talk about it if he didn't want to. However, I did my best to help him face the reality of his situation. I would talk about God's supportive love that sees us through our darkest days and helps us face anything that confronts us. Reading the eighth chapter of Romans, stressing that not even death has the power to separate us from that love, became a ritual in our visits. When Steve asked for the twenty-third Psalm, I emphasized the Phrase, "though I walk through the valley of the shadow of death, I will fear no evil." I prayed with him that he might be able to accept the deterioration of his body and his impending death.

As with most of us, Steve had difficuly understanding God's love and grace. He felt that because he had neglected the church and lived out his days without any reference to God, he had to find something in his past that would merit such love. "We know that we have passed from death unto life, because we love the brethren" (1 John 3:14) was the only scripture he knew that offered him any hope.

"I've loved the brethren," he would say almost defensively after we had prayed together.

Steve would telephone me in between visits, so I was not surprised when he called that Thursday morning. I was surprised when he ordered me to be at his home at four o'clock that afternoon.

"What's happening at four?" I inquired.

"We are going to have a healing service."

"Who is we?"

"My daughter has arranged for her minister to be here to put his hands on me and heal me, and I want you here."

I knew that pastor had visited Steve. He and I had chatted at ministerial association meetings about Steve's condition and his daughter's involvement in the life of that neighboring congregation. I called him immediately.

"John, what kind of healing service are you having for Steve this afternoon?"

"His daughter is convinced that he can be healed, and that the laying on of hands will do it."

"But what about Steve?" I pleaded. "What will this do to him and his faith?"

"I don't know," he answered, "but I've got to do this to satisfy her."

Within minutes the telephone rang and Mrs. Stone expressed her distress about the plans for that afternoon.

"Can you come earlier to talk with Steve before our daughter and her pastor get here?"

I was there earlier but Steve's mind was made up. He was anticipating a healing miracle that afternoon and there was no way to convince him that an even greater miracle was already taking place in his life.

"Steve, you are more aware of God than you have been in all

your seventy years. Your sickness has made you receptive to God's love for you. That love will see you through anything, even your dying."

He could not hear me. There was no way for me to stop what was about to happen, for Steve's daughter was a very determined person and this had been her home at one time and he was her father. Even Mrs. Stone could not prevent it.

I kept close to Steve's bed as the clergyman talked about the healing power of faith.

"If you have faith," he declared to Steve, "if you have faith, you will be healed by the touch of my hands."

I wanted to believe that as much as Steve, as much as his wife and daughter did. However, I knew what was happening to Steve's lungs, and I knew that eventually he would drown in the fluid from the tumor. I knew he was going to die. I was trying, as his pastor and his friend, to help him face death believing firmly in God's love for him.

John and I left the house together.
"How could you do that?" I asked him.
"The old man needed hope and I gave him hope."

That afternoon I felt as helpless as Jeremiah must have felt when he could make no response to the preaching of the prophet Hananiah.

Jeremiah had tried to help the Judean king, Zedekiah, realize that his country would soon be completely taken over by the Babylonians. An alliance with her small neighboring countries could not stop the inevitable. Any attempt the Judeans made to resist Babylon would cause them to suffer more. Jeremiah knew that the only way his country could survive was by submitting to Babylon.

The king, however, was under the influence of a group of prophets who constantly assured him that the Babylonians could not conquer Judah, and that the brass vessels recently taken from the temple by those invaders would soon be back in Yahweh's house.

In an effort to convince the king and the Judean people that submission was their only course, Jeremiah made a wooden yoke to wear on his neck. One day in the temple he was confronted by Hananiah who claimed that the Lord had said to him, "I have broken the power of the king of Babylonia, within two years I will bring back . . . all the temple treasures . . . and all the people of Judah who went into exile in Babylonia." (28:2-3, TEV)

"Wonderful! I hope the Lord will do this! I certainly hope he will make your prophecy come true!'' was Jeremiah's response to Hananiah.(28:6, TEV)

All I could say that afternoon was, ''John, I hope Steve will get well.''

Hananiah took the yoke off Jeremiah's neck and broke it. He said to the people, ''The Lord has said this is how he will break the yoke that King Nebuchadnezzar has put on the neck of all the nations.'' (28:10, TEV)

Jeremiah did not try to prove that he was right and Hananiah was wrong. He did not call down a curse on his opponent. All he could do was walk away.

All I could do that Thursday was to express my hope and leave.

Are you troubled by the silence of God? I am. John spoke with real authority that afternoon. I have never felt I had such authority. When others seem so sure of their communication with the Lord, I feel disturbed because I am met only with silence. Hananiah sounded a lot more religious than Jeremiah, and certainly more official. He spoke ''in the house of the Lord, in the presence of the priest and all the people.'' Moreover, he said what the people wanted to hear. John spoke with authority and said what Steve and his daughter wanted to hear.

Jesus was in the same position as Jeremiah. All the religious hierarchy stood opposite him. The priests opposed him because he upset not only their hope, but also their whole pious organization. They were eagerly waiting for a Messiah who would liberate them from Roman occupation, and yet Jesus would not start a war against the Romans by sword or by miracle. Apparently powerless and helpless, he let himself be crucified. God's silence was awesome, unbearable that day in A.D 30. His Son was crucified, and God was silent. The sky didn't open. No angels descended. Scoffers stood by and mocked. Those who had traveled with Jesus did not understand such silence, so they left.

We all want to have our hopes fulfilled. That's what makes it easy for us to listen to prophets who cut their pattern to fit our cloth. Both Hananiah and Jeremiah spoke in the name of Yahweh. To all outward appearance there was no way to tell which was the true prophet. Hananiah understood that Israel's election meant privilege. Jeremiah had a vision of God which demanded responsibility and obedience. It has been a mistake, frequently a tragic mistake, of ''religious'' people down through the centuries who, like Hananiah, have all too often confused their own beliefs and aspirations with the will of God. All people of profound faith, including Jeremiah and other great prophets, have had to learn to wait upon God, to endure the silence.

We must believe that time will always tell us that God's word, whether we like it or not, is real, genuine, and powerful. If we live with it, we will discover it to be self-authenticating.

Why did God let Israel be defeated?

Why did God allow Jesus to be crucified?

Why does God permit cancer?

These are hard questions and we have no easy answers — and often no explanations.

Jeremiah assured his people that God would be with them in their exile and that his presence would sustain them even as they submitted to the Babylonian yoke. Calvary's ending was incredible, for Jesus the crucified rose on Easter day. And Steve, even though he was not healed, was assured that God loved him even as he died.

If only we would trust the silence . . .

The word of the Lord came to me again: "What do you mean by repeating this proverb concerning the land of Israel, 'The fathers have eaten sour grapes, and the children's teeth are set on edge'? As I live, says the Lord God, this proverb shall no more be used by you in Israel. Behold, all souls are mine; the soul of the father as well as the soul of the son is mine: the soul that sins shall die.

"If a man is righteous and does what is lawful and right — if he does not eat upon the mountains or lift up his eyes to the idols of the house of Israel, does not defile his neighbor's wife or approach a woman in her time of impurity, does not oppress any one, but restores to the debtor his pledge, commits no robbery, gives his bread to the hungry and covers the naked with a garment, does not lend at interest or take any increase, witholds his hand from iniquity, executes true justice between man and man, walks in my statutes, and is careful to observe my ordinances — he is righteous, he shall surely live, says the Lord God.

"Yet you say, 'The way of the Lord is not just.' Hear now, O house of Israel: Is my way not just? Is it not your ways that are not just? When a righteous man turns away from his righteousness and commits iniquity, he shall die for it; for the iniquity which he has committed he shal die. Again, when a wicked man turns away from the wickedness he has committed and does what is lawful and right, he shall save his life. Because he considered and turned away from all the transgressions which he had committed, he shall surely live, he shall not die. Yet the house of Israel says, 'The way of the Lord is not just.' O house of Israel, are my ways not just? Is it not your ways that are not just?"

(Ezekiel 18:1-9, 25-29)

If Only We Would Confess . . .

Someone had slipped a church bulletin under the study door. When I spotted it after the morning worship service and saw some notations on it, I assumed that the writer had jotted down an announcement or a date to be included in the newsletter that was to go to press Monday morning. Reading the note scrawled across the ritual, I knew it was meant, not for the newsletter, but for me.

"Garbage!" the note read. "This is garbage and we will not tolerate any more of it."

That note of judgment was not aimed at the service in general, but only part of it. The unidentified writer was neither disagreeing with my interpretation of Scripture, nor any of the content of the sermon, nor even the hymns selected for the service. The note was written across the congregational prayer of confession and certain phrases of that prayer were underlined.

I was not too surprised because, since coming to serve that congregation, I had heard rumblings about those confessional prayers; they were too specific, too pointed. The prayer that November morning went like this:

O God, your will and purpose for us is far finer, far greater, than we ever dared to hope. What bothers us deeply is not so much our sin, but our shabbiness; the poor use we have made of great gifts, the talents squandered, the resources unrealized.

We apologize for being so unbusinesslike about the business of living; for being so slipshod about the act of living.

We beg your pardon for being satisfied with getting instead of

getting on; for lazy prayers and slack speech; for half-hearted friend-
ships; for tired marriages.

We think with shame of uninvested wealth, of physical and men-
tal and spiritual capital that promoted nothing but our own secu-
rity, and brought nothing into being.

We ask forgiveness for silly sins like vanity, for weak sins like
self-pity, for shoddy sins like self-indulgence.

But above all, we pray to be pardoned for our lukewarm com-
mitment to Jesus Christ; for living, not by his truth, but by our
own preferences. Help us to commit our lives to the Lord of life,
to his way of thinking, acting, being.

When Jerusalem was captured by Babylonian forces in 597 B.C., the city was left intact, but the king and certain other leading citizens were taken to the captors' homeland. Among those refugees was a young priest named Ezekiel. While exiled in Babylon, Ezekiel saw a vision of God during a thunderstorm. He was commanded to tell his people what God intended to do with them and why. Up until the time of the second Hebrew deportation to Babylon and the destruction of the temple in 587 B.C., Ezekiel chastised his people for their unfaithfulness to God and foretold the doom of those remaining in Jerusalem and the land of Judah.

Like his prophetic predecessors, Ezekiel made it plain that God did not desire the doom and destruction that the Hebrews were facing. With anguished cry Ezekiel says in the name of Yahweh, "Why do you Israelites want to die?" (18:31, TEV) The covenant had been broken. God had been faithful and the people had been unfaithful; therefore, destruction was inevitable.

The Hebrews thought that their suffering in exile was the result of another generation's unfaithfulness to the covenant. They repeated the proverb, "The parents ate the sour grapes, but the children got the sour taste." (18:2, TEV) They thought of themselves as innocent victims, thus shifting the blame for the tragedy of exile to the previous generation.

God, speaking through Ezekiel, says, "You will not repeat this proverb in Israel any more. The life of every person belongs to me, the life of the parent as well as that of the child. The person who sins is the one who will die." (18:3-4, TEV)

Ezekiel ministered to the people in exile in addition to delivering oracles of doom to the nation of Judah. In chapter eighteen he tried to help his people see that, in spite of where one was or how one got into that situation, one could still be loyal to Yahweh and keep his commands. If so, that person would have a good and wholesome life. If not, that person would destroy himself or herself by not being obedient to God's requirements. The clear indication was that the individual was expected to repent and remain faithful to God no matter what the circumstances.

Ezekiel became very specific about what constituted the good life. "A truly good man . . . doesn't worship idols . . . doesn't seduce another man's wife or have intercourse with a woman during her period . . . doesn't cheat or rob anyone . . . returns what a borrower gives him as security . . . refuses to do evil and gives an honest decision in any dispute." (18:5-8, TEV) He then points out that the man who robs and kills, seduces other men's wives, cheats the poor, worships idols, and such other disgusting things does not live a good life and is responsible for his doom.

Ezekiel, as God's spokesman, tried to help his people understand that every individual should fulfill within himself or herself the covenant requirements. He could have spoken in general terms, telling the people to obey God's commands and keep God's laws. He could have said, "Stop sinning and do what is right." But Ezekiel pointed out specific sins, which must have been as disturbing to the Hebrews as that prayer of confession was to the worshiper.

Confessing our sins is difficult. Confession demands honesty. Confession must be specific. It is easy to ask God to forgive our many sins. It is painful to confess particular sins like pride and envy, anger and lust, and then feel worthy of forgiveness. We usually take a rather bland view of our conduct, preferring to congratulate ourselves on our virtues rather than dwelling much on our failures. Those who talk about being sinners in need of forgiveness are unwelcomed. They are like one who persistently calls attention to the fact that there is something wrong with the drains, when the other people living in the house would prefer to ignore the rather strange smells they can't help noticing from time to time, and find it much more congenial to maintain that everything is in order.

A Christian is a realist. He or she should continue to insist that everything is very far from being in order, that try as we will to live in a world of pretense, the brute fact of sin is an inescapable one which all of us must face and take into account. To ignore the existence of sin is to refuse to face up to reality. This, psychologists say, is fatal to mental health.

We cannot begin to deal with anything until we identify it. If we refuse to identify our sinfulness we deceive ourselves. If we cannot or will not tolerate the pain of self-examination, we hinder our ability to make confession. We get to a point where the mirror of our lives reflects only righteousness to us. If we do anything to avoid the pain that comes from looking honestly at ourselves, we eventually will hate the light of goodness that shows us up, or the light of scrutiny that exposes us, or the light of truth that penetrates our deception.

The Israelites had hard times with their prophets, especially those whose messages spoke doom to the tiny kingdoms of Judah and Israel, and of the part that the people were playing in bringing about that doom. They were usually successful in ignoring these unpleasant messengers, but there were so many of them and they spoke with such persistence that they proved to be nuisances. As long as the prophets spoke in generalities and as long as difficulties could be explained away as the corporate commmunity's fault, the people let the prophets carry on. It was when thay became specific, as did Amos and Jeremiah and Ezekiel, that the listeners tried to silence their messages.

The congregational prayer of confession was, perhaps, too specific, but I have discovered in my personal life that I must be precise and definite when I pray, especially when I ask forgiveness for my sins.

Most of us are like William Temple, the late Archbishop of Canterbury. As a student at Oxford University, he went to hear a famous American evangelist. The preacher talked about the forgiveness of God, quoting the Isaiah text, "Through your sins be as scarlet, they shall be as white as snow." (1:18) Dr. Temple writes:

> *Though I went to that meeting in a serious, inquiring spirit, I found myself quite unmoved, for alas, my sins were not scarlet, they were gray, all gray. They were not dramatic acts of rebellion, but the colorless, tired sins of omission, inertia, and timidity.*

Twenty years ago I took a course in pastoral care at a state institution for the mentally ill. Each Monday for eleven weeks, two other ministers and I made the trip for a full day of classes. In addition to the class work, we were required to write six papers, read three books, and take a final examination. I fulfilled all the requirements, with the exception of reading all of one book, *An Elementary Textbook of Psychoanalysis.* I simply did not get it done on time, but made up my mind that I would finish it. I justified it all to myself when I reported having done everything. I carried that gray sin, that failure with me for years. I lied. I reported having done something I did not do. It wasn't a monstrous, scarlet sin. I could have convinced myself that every time I prayed for forgiveness for my sins of omission, that gray one was included and forgiven. Strange to say, I only felt real forgiveness when I openly confessed that particular sin in a sermon on forgiveness.

Keith Miller, an Episcopal layman, has written a number of books on commitment. In *The Second Touch,* he tells how sharing himself with his family through prayer led to a kind of openness. For a long time he and his wife had a standard prayer ritual with their children at bedtime. It consisted of "Now I lay me down to sleep," followed by the God blesses. One night Mr. Miller was going through this ritual with his five-year old daughter when he realized he wasn't praying at all with his child. They had never heard any confession or petition from him about the things that were real in his life.

The next evening he came home irritated about something that happened at work, and at the dinner table he took out his irritation on the family, speaking sharply to Mrs. Miller and the children. That night, as he was tucking the same five-year-old into bed, he began the prayer. "Dear God, forgive me for being so fussy at dinner tonight." There was a kind of awed silence. Then very quickly, his little girl went through the familiar "Now I lay me" and the usual God blesses.

The next night it happened that Mr. Miller was again irritable when he came home and showed his irritation at dinner. As he was having his nightly ritual with his daughter, he prayed, "Dear Lord, forgive me for being so cross again tonight and help me not to be fussy. I really don't want to be that way. Please help me to try hard not to be."

There was the same silence. Then, with eyes clenched shut, his little girl very quickly prayed: "Dear God, forgive me for tee teeing out in the backyard under the tree last summer." That was real confession for that five-year-old, and as specific as her father's.

If only you and I would be as willing to confess . . .

The word of the Lord came to me: "Son of man, speak to your people and say to them, If I bring the sword upon a land, and the people of the land take a man from among them, and make him their watchman; and if he sees the sword coming upon the land and blows the trumpet and warns the people; then if any one who hears the sound of the trumpet does not take warning, and the sword comes and takes him away, his blood shall be upon his own head. He heard the sound of the trumpet, and did not take warning; his blood shall be upon himself. But if he had taken warning, he would have saved his life. But if the watchman sees the sword coming and does not blow the trumpet, so that the people are not warned, and the sword comes, and takes any one of them; that man is taken away in his iniquity, but his blood I will inquire at the watchman's hand.

"So you, son of man, I have made a watchman for the house of Israel; whenever you hear a word from my mouth, you shall give them warning from me. If I say to the wicked, O wicked man, you shall surely die, and you do not speak to warn the wicked to turn from his way, that wicked man shall die in his iniquity, but his blood I will require at your hand. But if you warn the wicked to turn away from his way, and he does not turn from his way; he shall die in his iniquity, but you will have saved your life.

"And you, Son of man, say to the house of Israel, Thus have you said: 'Our transgressions and our sins are upon us, and we waste away because of them; how can we live?' Say to them, As I live, says the Lord God, I have no pleasure in the death of the wicked, but that the wicked turn back from his way and live; turn back, turn back from your evil ways; for why will you die, O house of Israel?"

(Ezekiel 33:1-11)

Ezekiel 33:1-11

If Only We Would Accept Responsibility . . .

"Are you the minister?" he asked as I came through the court-yard toward the entrance of the church. I wanted to say no, because there were dozens of things that needed my attention that Monday morning when I got to work.

With a bit of dumb resentment at the interruption of my planned agenda, I acknowledged that I was one of the pastors of that down-town church. He followed me into the office complex.

"What can I do for you?" I asked, hoping that a meal ticket or perhaps a quick referral to another helping agency of the city would suffice.

"God is sending me to Florida and I need a bus ticket," he replied.

I usually steered away from any theological discussions with tran-sients who came by our church, but I couldn't resist this one. I was tempted to ask him why God had made no provisions for his jour-ney, but fought back the impulse, remembering Abram's instruc-tions to start out to Canaan. (Genesis 12:1)

My inquiries brought some conflicting answers from my visitor.

"Where were you living when God gave you instructions to go to Florida?"

"In Farmville, Virginia."

"With whom?" I continued.

First, he said, he was staying with friends and God told him the friends didn't want him there any longer, so he left.

"Is that when you were told to go to Florida?" I asked.

"No," he answered. "I then went to live with my parents in Farmville. They did not approve of my marriage to a divorced woman with a child."

"Oh, you are married! Where are your wife and stepchild, and why aren't you living with them?"

This time it was the devil who had spoken to him, advising him to make up his mind whether or not to go back to his wife.

"What did you decide?"

His final instructions came from God, who told him to divorce his wife, and take this trip to Florida.

"God is in my head deciding everything for me to do!" he declared. "I follow his instructions, and do everything he tells me."

I couldn't let that theological statement go by unchallenged. After another twenty minutes of hearing him shift responsibility for his decisions to God and "the devil" (elsewhere), I confronted him with his refusal to assume responsibility for himself. That didn't sit too well with him. He became angry and verbally defrocked me.

"You're no minister if you don't believe that God directs me! He told me to get money from you to go to Florida, but you won't listen to God! I'll go find someone who does listen, as I do!"

He left without a bus ticket to Florida, but I hope he had begun to think about his need to accept responsibility for his life and his decisions.

The telephone rang at one o'clock in the morning at a minister's home. As he reached to answer it, his mind raced through his list of hospital patients. A late call usually meant critical illness or death, but this call was from the police. The church's security system had alerted the police, and they asked the pastor to meet them at the church. By the time he arrived, a "visitor" had been apprehended as he was leaving the building. He was carrying a bag of tools and one door showed the marks of his crowbar.

"What were you doing in there?" a police officer demanded.

Holding his bag of burglar's tools, the thief replied, "I broke in to pray. That's what God told me to do."

"You can try that out on the judge, but as far as I'm concerned we caught you red-handed," the officer responded as he handcuffed the thief and led him to the patrol car.

The writer of the third chapter of Genesis tells us that Adam and Eve were caught "red-handed." When they were, they did what the transient and the burglar did. The transient and the burglar made God and "the devil" responsible for their actions. When Adam and Eve could not pretend they were innocent, they, too, tried to shift the blame for their disobedience.

Adam protested at first that God was responsible, because it was God's idea to create a helpmate. "The woman you put here with me . . . " he began. (Genesis 3:12, TEV) If anyone were to be held responsible for Adam's disobedience, God must stand first in line, Adam seemed to be saying.

Adam then pointed the guilty finger at Eve. " . . . she gave me the fruit, and I ate it." (Genesis 3:12, TEV) Because Eve was the first to eat, she set the standard and tempted him, Adam reasoned. Since the fruit was given to him and he had not sought it, Eve was responsible for his sin.

Eve was not without her defense. The serpent was responsible for her disobedience. The Lord asked her, "Why did you do this?" She replied, "The snake tricked me into eating it." (Genesis 3:13, TEV)

Like the transient and the burglar, these representatives of humankind were shifting responsibility for their actions somewhere else. It was God's fault. It was Eve's fault. It was the snake's fault. This early biblical writer lets us see how humankind, from its very beginning, has refused to take responsibility for itself. You and I are no exception.

Five-hundred-fifty years before the birth of Jesus, the whole middle eastern world was ruled by Babylon, a ruthless and barbaric nation. The tiny kingdom of Judah fell when King Jehoiachin surrendered to the Babylonian armies of Nebuchadrezzer in 589 B.C. All her artists, her merchants, her prophets had been systematically removed from their beloved country and resettled along the Euphrates River. The chosen people were in exile.

Among those deported from Jerusalem to Babylon was a young priest named Ezekiel. For five years he witnessed the life of his exiled people and, in a vision, saw his nation finally destroyed, even, to his horror, the holy city and the temple.

Throughout Ezekiel's prophecy runs the theme of the individual's responsibility to fulfill the covenant requirements and the inevitable results of refusing to do so. The idea of individual responsibility was not new with Ezekiel, but it had often been overshadowed by the older concept of the corporate responsibility of the covenant community. So long as the people of God were physically present in Israel and Judah, the prophets spoke of the nation and the people as a corporate personality. Although Ezekiel does not solve the knotty problem of inherited guilt (18:2), he *does* conclude that the individual is responsible before God. How could it be otherwise, he must have reasoned, since the visible covenant community was disintegrating and any subsequent faithfulness to God must lie with the individual.

Ezekiel illustrated his point by using the familiar figure of a watchman, posted outside the city to warn the inhabitants of approaching invaders. Each individual citizen was responsible to heed the trumpet call of the watchman; if he paid no attention and was overtaken by the enemy, he was responsible for his own fate. If the watchman failed to give a warning, he was to be held responsible for those killed by the invaders.

Ezekiel was keenly aware that he had been called to be God's watchman, to be a messenger to warn the Israelites of impending destruction for those who did not give up their evil ways. The twofold responsibility of God's messenger and those to whom he was sent is clearly spelled out by this Old Testament prophet.

How often have you and I blamed God for some of the things that happen to us, even some of the things we do? If I am poor and I steal, it is God's fault for setting up a world in which there is poverty. If I am sexually irresponsible, I might ask, "Well, God, if this is wrong, why did you make me a sexual being?" We may become more sophisticated and blame our horoscopes. Is it because we want to believe that our lives are guided and destined by the planets, or the stars, or other celestial objects over which we have no control? If we believe that, we can breathe a sigh of relief and declare that we can't help the way we are since our lives are determined by Zodiac signs. And so it goes, on and on, and we even come back to the ultimate responsibility of the God who made the stars.

A Presbyterian minister was called to the hospital early one morning. The wife and daughter of a member of his church had both been killed in an automobile accident. The son, in critical condition, was in surgery. A nurse came to the husband and father with what she thought were comforting words. "It is hard to understand the ways of God. I know it is hard for you to understand why God did this."

The minister said that statement made his adrenalin flow, even though it was five o'clock in the morning. "Sister," he said, "God was not driving that other automobile. A drunk was. God was not tending the bar when that man got drunk. An irresponsible bartender was. Let's not hear any nonsense about God doing this. Acts of sinful men caused this tragedy."

When we have messed up our lives we, like the transient and the burglar, like Adam and Eve, want to blame someone or something besides ourselves. We are responsible for what we do. Ezekiel tried to say this to his people, to convince each individual of his or her responsibility for keeping the covenant.

We laugh when Flip Wilson, the television comedian, says, "The devil made me do it," but that comment expresses a widespread belief that some outside force is responsible for the evil in the world. We cannot bear to think that it springs from within us. That essentially is what was said an one of the highest courtrooms in America when Richard Nixon's chief aide, Alexander Haig, was testifying in Judge Sirica's court. He was explaining why there was an eighteen-minute gap in one of the Watergate tapes. It was, he said, the result of some "evil sinister force."

The moral standards of our society, as of Ezekiel's, are threatened by our refusal to be accountable for our actions. Actually, Haig's "evil sinister force" has become the scapegoat for a number of us who claim to be Christian. Our sins, we declare, are not our own. "The devil made me do it." This always sounds as if we are baing forced to act against our own will. If something goes wrong in our lives, we claim that it is the "devil" trying to destroy our pet enterprise.

"If someone hears it (the alarm) but pays no attention and the enemy comes and kills him, then he is to blame for his own death," God said to Ezekiel. (33:4) We have heard that we make our own choices and we cannot blame anyone or anything else when those choices are irresponsible or evil. Neither can we escape the consequences. Ezekiel, the watchman, has told us. Christ, the Lord, has told us.

We have also heard that when we accept responsibility for our choices, and repent, the waiting God eagerly forgives us, and our eternal relationship with God is restored and deepened.

If only we would accept responsibility . . .

Hear the word of the Lord, O
    people of Israel;
for the Lord has a controversy
    with the inhabitants of the land.
There is no faithfulness or kindness,
    and no knowledge of God in the land;
there is swearing, lying, killing,
    stealing, and committing adultery;
    they break all bounds and murder follows
murder.
Therefore the land mourns,
    and all who dwell in it languish,
and also the beasts of the field,
    and the birds of the air;
    and even the fish of the sea are taken away.
I will return again to my place,
    until they acknowledge their guilt and seek my
face,
    and in their distress they seek me, saying,
    "Come, let us return to the Lord,   for he has
torn, that he may heal us;
    he has stricken, and he will bind us up.
After two days he will revive us;
    on the third day he will raise us up,
    that we may live before him.
Let us know, let us press on to know the Lord;
    his going forth is sure as the dawn;
he will come to us as the showers,
    as the spring rains that water the earth."
What shall I do with you, O Ephraim?
    What shall I do with you, O Judah?
Your love is like a morning cloud,
    like the dew that goes early away.
Therefore I have hewn them by the prophets,
    I have slain them by the words of my mouth,
    and my judgment goes forth as the light.
For I desire steadfast love and not sacrifice,
    the knowledge of God, rather than burnt
offerings.

(Hosea 4:1-3, 5:15—6:6)

Hosea 4:1-3, 5:15-16:6

Proper 19 (C)
Pentecost 17 (L)
Ordinary Time 24 (RC)

If Only We Could Be Loyal . . .

Jackie had been at our worship service on only two occasions, and when she came to me for counseling, I began by saying, "Tell me who you are." We spent over an hour talking about her, for my sole contact with her had been from the pulpit to the pew, an introduction, and a handshake.

Jackie felt that her whole life was deteriorating. It began when her father abandoned his family and she watched her mother struggle for years to provide a home for her and her sister. Endowed with a brilliant mind, Jackie did well in high school, and a wealthy couple in that small town had provided money for her college education.

"In college, things began to fall apart," she continued her story. It seemed that she was incapable of maintaining any lasting relationships. She had trouble with roommates and faculty members, and became such a disturbing force on the school's rifle team that a dismissal was the only course the instructor could take. That was the crowning blow. She withdrew from college and spent six months in California, living with her married sister and working as a waitress.

"I had gone to college because that's what everyone expected me to do, and the couple even financed it. After the California experience, I returned to school because it was what I wanted and I could manage it financially." Jackie did well in school and, obviously, in her relationships, for she and a fellow student were married during their senior year.

Things didn't go well, however, at work. She had frequent clashes with her fellow employees and became estranged from some of them. She was fired, a devastating blow to her self-image. Then her marriage began to deteriorate. She and her husband separated, and it may all end in divorce. In her loneliness she has taken a lover, but that relationship promises no permanence. The father who abandoned her tried to enter her life again, but she would not allow it, because of the bitterness she had carried all through childhood and into her young adult years.

I looked at my watch and realized that two hours had gone by. It was time for Jackie to leave. That's when I asked her why she had come to me. "Because you represent a force in life that I have neglected for years. I had problems in high school, but could cope with them because of my close association with the church and with God. I've neglected that strength over the past twelve years. If only I had held tightly to it, I would be able to cope better — would *be* better. That's why I am here."

The next three months of counseling with Jackie and her husband made it clear that money, recreation, religion, and sex had been the four elements that had been distorted or neglected in their marriage. Paul, the husband, re-echoed his wife's feeling that she was unable to cope because of having neglected faith: he had not only neglected the faith, he had also dismissed it.

It was in the late afternoon, as the autumn sun was casting shadows over falling leaves that I hear his plaintive cry: "I wish we could go back and start over again. I wish our allegiance to God had been top priority for us."

Those haunting words were back. "If only . . . "

Every time I read through the Book of Judges in the Old Testament, it makes me wonder if the people of Israel didn't often cry, like Jackie's husband, "If only we had been more loyal . . ." You recall the formula that runs through the story of each judge. The nation, when it began to enjoy a period of prosperity, neglected its faith. When adversity and disaster came, the people were immediately convinced that this was the result of their neglect. So they prayed for a deliverer, a hero who would call them back to their first loyalty. The lesson of this biblical book is that Israel's survival depended on her loyalty to God, that her neglect always led to disaster. But there was more than this: even when the nation forgot God and disaster came, God was always ready to save his people when they repented and turned to him again.

Jackie and her husband are much like the people of Israel. Both had been reared in the church. During their childhood and adolescence, they had been introduced to the faith, had made commitments, and offered themselves in service. Jackie had been a leader in her Baptist church youth group, and worship each Sunday was a routine part of her life. Her husband grew up as part of the Lutheran Church and related the satisfaction that serving as an acolyte had given him. Both became aware of how they had drifted away during their twenties because everything was going fairly well. It was only when the disaster of their failure in marriage became evident that they turned again to find the strength of their faith.

Hosea was one of those Old Testament prophets who carefully examined Israel's past and told his people about it. (7:8-11; 7:13-16) He also looked carefully at the present situation, telling the Hebrews what they were doing wrong and why they should change their ways. (4:1-2; 7:1-2) Finally, like those other prophetic spokesmen for God, Hosea proclaimed a sort of conditional future:

> *If the people of Israel will return to the Lord, he will bandage their wounds. He will come to them as surely as the day dawns, as surely as the spring rains upon the earth. (6:1-3)*

If there were no repentance and return, then "the land will dry up, and everything that lives on it will die." (4:1) Hosea pleaded with the people on God's behalf: "God only wants your loyalty, not your sacrifices." (6:6) He wants your love. God wants you to know him so that you can feel the depth of his love, a love that is strong in spite of your disloyalty, that doesn't disappear like mist and dew. If you persist in being disloyal, Hosea said, you will render God helpless and bring destruction on yourself.

Hosea's prophetic words were born out of his personal life. He could speak of the depth of God's covenant love because of his own love for a wife who rejected him. He knew that disloyalty broke God's heart, for *his* heart had been broken when the wife became unfaithful. This prophet knew he could not force Gomer, his wife, to change her ways, to return to her family, to accept the love they offered her. He could foresee only destruction unless she did change, the same darkness that stared his nation in the face if it continued its present waywardness.

Hosea's lessons are so powerful that they can either haunt us with their inevitability or help us in our relationship with God.

That relationship is based on convenant love. The people of

Israel had become "wedded" to God when they entered a convenant relationship with him on Mount Sinai. God had delivered them from Egyptian bondage, had taken care of their needs in the wilderness, and had led them to the promised land.

As Hosea observed his wife's unfaithfulness to him, he realized how unfaithful the people of Israel had been to God. Straying to other gods, they had neglected their vows of loyalty and faithfulness to the God of their fathers. Hosea began to plead with them to return, to repent, to renew their vows of covenant love. Jesus, too, spent much of his ministry pleading with persons to establish a firm commitment to God. Committed love was at the very center of his preaching. To express it, he used words like rebirth, renewal, repentance, redemption, salvation, grace, hope, healing. No matter what the language, the message was always the same: be true and faithful to God as you have promised him you would.

Jackie and her husband, realizing where they were in their marriage and in their lives, yearned to have listened to that same kind of plea, and responded. It could have prevented their lament, "If only we had been loyal . . . "

Hosea also portrays graphically that the covenant-love relationship with God is made possible by God's forgiveness. We prostitute our souls in sinfulness bit by bit. Our disloyalty is usually not an overnight failure, but a nibbling away at the commitment until it is gobbled up by incidentals, lesser loyalties, minor and secondary priorities.

God will never force us to be true to him. He will not prevent us from divorcing ourselves from him. He will not compel us to repent, to be loyal. God does, through Jesus, promise that his love and forgiveness are unending, unearned, unchanging. The invitation to return to God and be forgiven is constant.

I am convinced that this young couple is seeking God, for they both are aware of how far they have strayed from their first love. They are discovering a Father who is waiting for them, ready to forgive them and restore the covenant.

Our reaction to Hosea's prophecy can be a humbling experience. It is difficult to swallow our pride, crying out, "We, too, have gone our own way and forgotten God. If only we had been loyal!" To promise to follow Christ is a tremendous responsibility, but only keeping that promise offers hope and happiness. As in a happy marriage relationship, our covenant of committed love with God should grow and mature with each passing day and year.

Unfortunately, many married couples, like Jackie and her husband, take that relationship so for granted that it deteriorates from neglect. The same is true of our covenant with God. We begin, perhaps casually, to shift our loyalties elsewhere, and when we hit a snag or run into dificulties, we begin to realize what we have done, and cry, "If only . . . "

If only we had been loyal . . . The good news is that, regardless of what we have done, God will forgive us when we are unfaithful and help us with any problems life throws at us. Even when we divorce ourselves from him, he will take us back and help us to start over. I listened to Jackie and Paul confess their disloyalty and heard them make some promises to be loyal to God and to one another.

If we look at ourselves honestly and deeply, there is no way we can keep Hosea's homily from being personally written for us. Whether his message haunts us or helps us depends upon how we handle our covenant relationship with God and how we accept his forgiveness. Maybe the message which Hosea leaves with us is that God always invites us to return, to accept his offer of life, and to hope, no matter how far we have wandered or how disloyal we have been.

If only we will renew our covenant, and be loyal to it . . .

When Israel was a child, I loved him,
    and out of Egypt I called my son.
The more I called them,
    the more they went from me;
they kept sacrificing to the Baals,
    and burning incense to idols.
Yet it was I who taught Ephraim to walk,
    I took them up in my arms;
    but they did not know that I healed them.
I led them with cords of compassion,
    with the bands of love,
and I became to them as one
    who eases the yoke on their jaws,
    and I bent down to them and fed them.
They shall return to the land of Egypt,
    and Assyria shall be their king,
    because they have refused to return to me.
The sword shall rage against their cities,
    consume the bars of their gates,
    and devour them in their fortresses.
My people are bent on turning away from me;
    so they are appointed to the yoke,
    and none shall remove it.
How can I give you up, O Ephraim!
    How can I hand you over, O Israel!
How can I make you like Admah!
    How can I treat you like Zeboiim!
My heart recoils within me,
    my compassion grows warm and tender.
I will not execute my fierce anger,
    I will not again destroy Ephraim;
for I am God and not man,
    the Holy One in your midst,
    and I will not come to destroy.
They shall go after the Lord,
    he will roar like a lion;
yea, he will roar,
    and his sons shall come trembling from the west;
they shall come trembling like birds from Egypt,
    and like doves from the land of Assyria;
    and I will return them to the homes,
        says the Lord.

(Hosea 11:1-11)

If Only We Could Remember . . .

On the back page of our capitol city's daily newspaper there are two columns headed "Divorces Filed" and "Divorces Granted." Sometimes when I glance at that back page and see the lists, I read through the names, and I wonder what kind of stories lie behind them. What happened to John and Cathy, to Bill and Sue, to Joe and Betty? I can almost picture the high moments in their lives as they made plans for their weddings, almost sense all the expectations that they carried into their marriages. Now, because of disillusionment, disenchantment, distrust, disloyalty, disagreement, dissatisfaction, those pledges of faith and those vows of love are shattered. The commitment, the covenant they made on their wedding day has been broken. From their experiences we could glean bruisings, brokenness, bereavement. Their marriages have failed, and dealing with this fact cannot be easy. From some of these failures bitterness, backbiting, and betrayal have undoubtedly come.

The Bible tells us about a man whose marriage failed. In fact, one whole book in the Old Testament tells the story of this marriage and what the man learned from it.

We have only the first names of this couple, Hosea and Gomer. The short book goes by Hosea's name.

We know nothing about Hosea before his marriage. We do know that his experience within that marriage, with its failure and restoration, taught him a lot about God. His book reflects what he learned. In fact, we could say that his theology and his marriage were intertwined. Through the phases of his marital relationship, Hosea gained some new insights into the relationship between God and His people.

There are three phases of Hosea's marriage. The first includes the engagement, the honeymoon, and the early years. The second phase is the estrangement and the break. The final stage is the reconciliation and restoration. Let's look at these three phases and see how this Old Testament prophet's marriage affected his theology.

I.

The first phase is the engagement, the honeymoon, and the initial years. Hosea, a young man, married Gomer, his beloved. She is a charming girl, in spite of her name. The first years of their marriage are happy ones. Their companionship is rich. The vows they exchanged are fresh in their minds. They establish a good home and have three children. They learn to like each other as friends. And perhaps they adjust reasonably well to one another's quirks. Chances are that for a long time Hosea and Gomer continue the courtesies practiced during their engagement. This may have been one of those remarkable cases when he still opens the door for her and she thanks him, and he still stands when she enters the room and she acknowledges his presence. These two people love each other dearly and every action shows that love and respect.

As a theologian, reflecting on those first years together, Hosea begins to draw parallels between his relationship to Gomer, his wife, and God's relationship to Israel, his people.

He has given his heart to Gomer. God has given his heart to Israel.

Hosea has pledged his love to his wife. God has pledged his love to his people.

He made a commitment to Gomer. God made a covenant with Israel.

There is a bond between Hosea and Gomer. There is a bond between God and Israel.

In his book, Hosea envisions God as saying, "I will betroth you to myself for ever, betroth you in lawful wedlock with unfailing devotion to myself for ever; I will betroth you to myself to have and to hold, and you shall know the Lord." (2:19-20, NEB)

These prophetic words sound very much like the covenant in the wedding ritual: " . . . to have and to hold from this day forward . . . to comfort . . . to honor . . . to keep in sickness and in health

. . . to love and to cherish until death . . . "

If only we could remember the time when we first came to God, and made promises, took vows, and became acutely aware of God's kindness, mercy, and faithfulness . . .

II.

The second phase of Hosea's marriage and his theological reflection is the estrangement and the break, and the bitterness that followed.

Things changed between Hosea and Gomer. Gomer seeks love elsewhere. She commits adultery. Hosea tells us that she has one love affair after another. She rejects her husband. She thinks that a more exciting life can be found elsewhere. So she seeks entertainment without discrimination. She grows tired of her obligations, her responsibilities, her promises. She gives her allegiance to other men, men who use her and who, when they have finished using her, discard her. She goes from lover to lover, from allegiance to allegiance.

Hosea pleads with Gomer to give up her adulterous ways and come home. He sends the children to plead with their mother. But she sends word back to him: "I will go after my lovers; they give me my food and drink, my wool and flax, my oil and my perfumes." (2:5, NEB)

Out of that brokenness and rejection, Hosea the husband becomes Hosea the theologian. As he reflects on the way Gomer has rejected him, broken his heart, crushed his spirit, he sees that God's people have done the same thing to God. God, too, is the rejected husband. This is the phase of his marriage and his theology on which Hosea dwells the most in his book.

Hosea becomes outspoken about Israel's adultery. Much of what he says to the Israelities about their infidelity to God could be repeated without alteration from any American pulpit.

> There is no good faith or mutual trust,
> no knowledge of God in the land,
> oaths are imposed and broken, they kill and rob;
> there is nothing but adultery and licence,
> one deed of blood after another. (4:1-2)

New wine and old steal my people's wits:
they ask advice from a block of wood
and take their orders from a fetish;
for a spirit of wantonness has led them astray
and in their lusts they are unfaithful to their God. (4:12)

They make kings, but not by my will;
they set up officers, but without my knowledge;
they have made themselves idols of their silver and gold. (8:4)

Biblical scholars say that Israel was spoiled by success. The nation had come through difficult times in establishing itself in the new land. Now that the difficulties and hardships were over, and it was enjoying prosperity, Israel forgot that what it possessed was a gift from God and turned to heathen Gods. Hosea cried out: "Israel is like a rank vine ripening its fruit; his fruit grows more and more, and more and more his altars; the fairer his land becomes, the fairer he makes his sacred pillars." (10:1, NEB)

It is ironic, isn't it, that the more abundantly we are blessed, as individuals or as nations, the more prone we are to give credit to our own energy and ingenuity or to our democratic or capitalistic systems. If we experience difficulty or defeat, we call for help. If we prosper and are successful, we congratulate ourselves.

If only we could remember our relationship to God, and be faithful in it . . .

III.

Let's move to the third phase of this story: the reconciliation, the restoration, the renewal.

Hosea would have been justified in taking stern measures against Gomer. Any court would have granted him an immediate divorce. In fact, in those days and in the centuries to come, he could have commanded that Gomer be stoned to death for her adulterous ways. (Leviticus 20:14; John 8:1-5)

Gomer had injured Hosea deeply. She had exposed him to shame. She had torn apart the lives of her children. She deserved to be divorced, maybe even stoned to death. She had shown that she no longer loved her husband, that she had forgotten her promises and ignored her vows. Perhaps because of her age or disease or faded attractiveness, Gomer's latest lover had grown weary of her and put her up for sale in the slave market.

Hosea could have sat by and muttered, "Aha, maybe she has finally learned her lesson. I tried to warn her, but she wouldn't listen. I could have told her it would eventually end up like this. She's reaping what she has sown. She has gotten what she deserves. I hope she suffers all the heartache she imposed on me and the children."

Instead, he goes down to the slave market and waits there until auction time. When they bring Gomer to the block, he weeps when he sees how she looks and what the years and her adulterous life have done to her. When the auctioneer asks for a bid, Hosea is the first bidder. He buys Gomer — not to be his slave, but to be his wife again. Although she has wronged him, made a mockery of their marriage, embarrassed him and the children, he brings her back into their home.

Now, for the third time, the prophet's marriage makes him stop and think about his theology. If his human love enables him to forgive Gomer's infidelity and take her back home, then the love of God, which is far more patient, infinitely more understanding, would surely forgive and restore. This is what the prophet sees and declares: God will forgive. Like Gomer, Israel will be accepted again as a partner in marriage.

Hosea has been called the prophet of grace. Long before he knew the generosity of God through Christ, he wrote:

> *How can I give you up, Ephraim,*
> *how surrender you, Israel?*
> *How can I make you like Admah*
> *or treat you as Zeboiim?*
> *My heart is changed within me,*
> *my remorse kindles already.*
> *I will not let loose my fury,*
> *I will not turn round and destroy Ephraim;*
> *for I am God and not a man,*
> *the Holy One in your midst;*
> *I will not come with threats like a roaring lion.*
> *No; when I roar, I who am God,*
> *my sons shall come with speed out of the west. (11:8-10)*

Through the medium of this Old Testament book, the merciful God reminds those of us who have slipped away from him, even those of us who have turned away, that he stands ready to renew our convenant relationship. He always stands ready, waiting to take us back. If only we could remember that!

Our God is not a God of wrath, ready to "zap" us for our unfaithfulness, but a God of love, calling us into oneness with him, into a relationship even more binding than marriage. Our fickle spirits too often corrupt this relationship, but even so, our God is still the God who stands ready to welcome us back, to buy us back, to renew the first commitment. It awes me to think of a God who could destroy us because we deserve it, yet who stoops down to beseech us, who waits for us to come home. If only we could remember that . . .

The closing words of Hosea's prophecy sound like the closing words of Jesus in the Sermon on the Mount: "Let the wise consider these things and let him who considers take note; for the Lord's ways are straight and the righteous walk in them, while sinners stumble." (14:9, NEB)

68

"Be glad, O sons of Zion,
    and rejoice in the Lord, your God;
for he has given the early rain for your vindication,
    he has poured down for you abundant rain,
    the early and the latter rain, as before.
"The threshing floors shall be full of grain,
    the vats shall overflow with wine and oil.
I will restore to you the years
    which the swarming locust has eaten.
the hopper, the destroyer, and the cutter,
    my great army, which I sent among you.
"You shall eat in plenty and be satisfied,
    and praise the name of the Lord your God,
    who has dealt wondrously with you.
And my people shall never again be put to shame.
You shall know that I am in the midst of Israel,
    and that I, the Lord, am your God
        and there is none else.
And my people shall never again be put to shame.
"And it shall come to pass afterward,
    that I will pour out my spirit on all flesh;
your sons and your daughters shall prophesy,
    your old men shall dream dreams,
    and your young men shall see visions.
Even upon the menservants and maidservants
    in those days, I will pour out my spirit.
    "And I will give portents in the heavens and on the
earth, blood and fire and columns of smoke."

                                (Joel 2:23-30)

Joel 2:23-30

Proper 21 (C)
Pentecost 19 (L)
Ordinary Time 26 (RC)

If Only We Would Be
Open To The Spirit . . .

Let's take some imaginary trips. I'd like us to picture ourselves going to a variety of places. As we go, I want us to listen carefully to what we hear.

First, we go to Reynolds Coliseum on the campus of North Carolina State University in Raleigh. We watch a basketball game. One of the Wolfpack players effectively manages to block a shot. We hear a fan call out, "That's the spirit!"

Now we're off to the football stadium on that same campus on a Saturday afternoon. Down on the field one particular play has gone exceedingly well, and the team is able to make a first down. If we could get into the huddle right after that play, we might hear the quarterback say to his teammates, "That's the spirit!"

Our next destination is a chemistry class at Raleigh's Broughton High School. One of the students, who is having difficulty understanding a formula, says to the teacher, "I'm going to lick this subject yet!" And the teacher replies, "That's the spirit!"

We now shift the scene to the physical therapy department at Rex Hospital. An elderly patient, recovering from a broken hip, is beginning to take those first tortured steps. Inevitably, the therapist or some fellow patient will call out, "That's the spirit!"

Let's sit in on a counseling session in which a married couple has succeeded in facing and handling some real problems in their life together. They voluntarily begin to re-negotiate and make some new commitments, and the counselor says, "That's the spirit!"

Here is a home where a man has been laid low by tragedy and failure. He is rising out of it with courage, managing to face life again and determined to pick up the pieces. Our response is the same: "That's the spirit!"

At the door of a church a worshipper says to the pastor, "The service today really spoke to my needs and gave me a new beginning." The pastor answers, "That's the spirit!"

From our brief observations we can see that we use the phrase. "That's the spirit!" in a variety of ways. This proves that it has many meanings. It can mean approval, achievement, accomplishment, or sanction, support, security. It may mean being alive, responsive, and vivacious. It often means being enthusiastic, animated, inspired. For Christians, it means the presence of God!

Not limited to our age, the expression, "That's the spirit," goes a long way back. If we pick up the Bible and read about early biblical times, we won't find these exact words, but we will find the writers saying basically the same thing.

The prophet Jeremiah had trouble with God's Spirit when He urged Jeremiah to be an unpopular spokesman for the truth. Jeremiah actually demanded that God release him from his ministry, a ministry that called him to say things he didn't want to say, to utter words he did not fully understand. He had grown weary of being God's mouthpiece, and yet he could not give up. When he tried to stop, he felt as if there were a fire smoldering within him, insistent on becoming a great blaze. "His word was in my heart like a fire, shut up in my bones." (20:9, TEV) That's the Spirit!

Ezekiel, another prophet, felt himself transported from one place to another by the Spirit of God. He said he could not understand his own words and movements. If we could have asked him why he said what he said and felt as he felt, he could certainly have answered, "That's the Spirit!"

Joel, one of the minor prophets of the Old Testament, perceives that Yahweh's greatest blessing would be Israel's "new age." The Spirit would usher in this golden era, assuring new life for all who call upon the name of the Lord, and destruction for those who turn away from God.

In his attempt to explain this concept, Joel powerfully and graphically describes how devastated the people of Judah were when a swarm of locusts swept across the land. The insects stripped trees and vines and left them bare, destroying not only the foliage, but also the plants themselves.

The locust plagues which struck Palestine usually came from the area south of Egypt. The insects deposited their eggs in the moist soil there and, when conditions were right, millions hatched, and, driven by hunger, moved across tha land, eating every green thing in sight. Joel is apparently describing an actual event, and his picture is so vivid that he may have seen it all for himself. He safely assumes that the people know exactly what he is talking about because they, too, were there.

Joel sees in this calamity something more than a natural phenomenon. To him, it is a warning of coming judgment, a sign of the impending "day of the Lord." (1:15) Like some of his prophetic predecessors, Joel felt that the "day of the Lord" was not to be a time when God would destroy evil nations and restore Israel, as Israel hoped. It was not a day to anticipate, because God's judgment would be directed against Israel as well as her enemies. Since God's people had become so unrighteous, God had no choice except to punish his chosen ones who ought to have known how to live, reasoned Joel.

Joel rings out his prophetic alarm all over the land so that the people will heed the locust plague as a clear warning from God. He calls for the nation to repent. If only the people of Israel will repent and return to the Lord in sincerity of heart, they will find him ready to forgive their past offenses (2:13) and bring in the new age they long for. It is described in one of Joel's most famous oracles:

> *I will pour out my spirit on everyone;*
> *your sons and daughters will proclaim my message;*
> *your old men will have dreams,*
> *and your young men will see visions.*
> *At that time I will pour out my spirit*
> *even on servants, both men and women.*
>
> *(2:28-29, TEV)*

For Joel, this outpouring of the Spirit of God is to be a future event. The Spirit is to be distributed without regard to age, sex, or social rank. Those who receive it will be enabled to discern God's will and interpret it to others. Moses had expressed his wish that God would put his Spirit on all the people of his day. (Numbers 11:29) Other prophets looked forward to an outpouring of the Spirit!

in messianic times (Isaiah 32:15; Ezekiel 39:29)

Jesus gathered his disciples in an upper room on the night before his death and made them witnesses to his last will and testament. He said, in essence, that part of the legacy he was leaving them was the Spirit. Five times around that table he reiterated the promise of the Spirit who would guide, inspire, and comfort them. Forty days later those disciples experienced that guidance, that inspiration, that comfort. "That's the Spirit!" they might have said to one another. Peter recalled Joel's oracle at Pentecost when he was trying to convince onlookers that the coming of Jesus had initiated the new age. (Acts 2:17-18)

We all have many personal feelings tied up with our belief about the movement of God's Spirit in our lives. Those feelings defy explanation. They are so private to some of us that it is impossible to share them with others. When I affirm my belief in God's Spirit, I am saying that I feel, I sense, I know that God is in the world and in my life.

Belief in God's Spirit means that God is not far from any one of us. It's comforting to know that God is near. It's also frightening to realize that he knows all my thoughts and sees all my acts. I believe that the permeating Spirit of God in the world means that no one of us is just a number, or just a member, or just a consumer, but that each of us has value because God never removes his Spirit from us.

I was taking my daughter and her friend back to college one Sunday afternoon. They were chatting about registering for the spring term and, as I was concentrating on driving, I caught only a part of their conversation.

I've already registered for that course, but I doubt if I'll get in because I'm in the seventies. You stand a good chance because you are right in the middle at forty-seven.

I inquired, "What do you mean seventy, forty-seven?"

The girls told me that the university students are known by the last four digits of their social security numbers. That's when I discovered that, according to the records and class schedule in Chapel Hill, I had reared student number 4719.

Sometimes, when I was in my study at my former church, I would get up from the desk and look out the rear window. There is always a steady stream of traffic and pedestrians in that downtown area. Spotting a car which had stopped for the traffic light, I would briefly wonder about the story behind the person driving that car. Seeing a government worker rushing across the street on some errand, I would wonder again. I marvel at our God whose Spirit hovers over each of them, and all of us.

It's so easy for us to rattle off statistics about abusers of alcohol and other drugs, unless our mate, or our parent, or our child happens to be among them. Then those statistics become painfully personal. The newspaper headlines may picture an airline crash in which over two-hundred people have perished. How casually we read about it, unless one of them is our relative, or our friend, or our acquaintance.

As Christians, when we say "that's the Spirit who cares for me and mine", we must realize that, as God cares for every statistic, so must we. God is not far from any one of us.

If only we would be open to that caring Spirit . . .

When I affirm my belief in God's Spirit, I also affirm the necessity of responding to God's presence. His Spirit is surrounding me, ready to instruct, guide, command, encourage, comfort, and inspire me, but I have to decide to acknowledge and answer to it. God takes the initiative, but the response is up to me.

John Killinger, in *Bread For The Wilderness, Wine For The Journey,* tells of a friend who kept a diary of her prayer life. She became convinced that she needed to be more disciplined in meditation and prayer. She decided to get up an hour earlier each day. She prayed, during that time, for others, friends, family, church members. Less than a month from the day she began to exercise that discipline, she wrote in her diary: "Our worship service was one of ecstasy! . . . the whole atmosphere was one of prayer. Wonder if my return to a daily communion with God has anything to do with it? I expect so." Dr. Killinger says that her journal shows that her whole life is permeated with God's Spirit. She decided to say "yes" to that Spirit.

I had an experience like that. The ministers in our area were expected to attend a three-day seminar, and even though it interfered with my routine and I wasn't very excited about the leader, I knew I should go. Before I left for the first session that Monday morning, I wrote in my own diary of private prayer: "In spite of my negative feelings about the seminar, I ask that I be open to all the possibilities." Before I left to attend Tuesday's session, I wrote in that same diary: "It astounds me to have prayer so readily answered. I asked for a good seminar yesterday and for receptivity. You helped me accomplish the latter, which made the first what it was." By God's grace, I responded to the Spirit.

The stained glass windows in a church I have served portray biblical characters. Enoch, Abraham, Isaiah, Peter, Paul are all there, as well as scenes from the life and ministry of Jesus. I used to marvel that those magnificent windows, which looked to me like colorless panels from the outside, took on brilliant colors once I was inside the sanctuary. Although the windows are the same outside and inside, they look entirely different, depending on where the observer stands.

It is the same with God's Spirit. If we let it, that Spirit can lead us into the interior of our lives where the windows of faith light up. That's where the new age dawns for us. Whenever that happens, "That's the Spirit!"

If only we would be open to the Spirit . . .

Notes

Notes

78

Notes

Notes

Notes